SO MANY QUESTIONS about... TRANSPORT

Sally Spray and Mark Ruffle

WAYLAND
www.waylandbooks.co.uk

First published in Great Britain in 2021 by Wayland
© Hodder and Stoughton Limited, 2021

HB ISBN: 978 1 5263 1761 2
PB ISBN: 978 1 5263 1762 9

Editor: Paul Rockett
Design and illustration: Mark Ruffle
www.rufflebrothers.com

MIX
Paper from
responsible sources
FSC
www.fsc.org
FSC® C104740

Printed in Dubai

Wayland
An imprint of Hodder Children's Group
Part of Hodder & Stoughton
Carmelite House
50 Victoria Embankment
London EC4Y 0DZ

An Hachette UK Company
www.hachette.co.uk
www.hachettechildrens.co.uk

Have you ever thought about transport? Think of all the questions you could ask ...

I have lots of questions for you.

Great! Let's investigate transport together ...

What is transport?

Transport is a word used to describe moving people or goods from one place to another. The machines used for transport are sometimes called vehicles. There are many different types, such as trains, ships and hot air balloons. What different types of transport can you see here?

There are more types of transport for travelling on land than by air or water. These include bicycles, buses, lorries, scooters and skateboards and your own two feet!

Think about ... the most popular kinds of transport.

Planes can transport you to another country much faster than a car, train or ship.

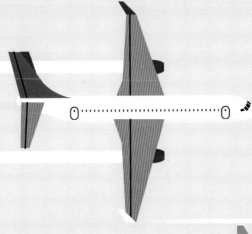

The fastest flight was made by the **North American X-15**. It flew at 7,200 km/h in 1967. This rocket-powered plane was launched from another plane mid-air.

Container ships transport food, fuel and other goods around the world. Some are over 400 m long – that's longer than the Eiffel Tower is tall!

Which forms of transport do you use?
Why do we need different types of transport?
Which is your favourite type of transport?

Which type of transport do you like least?
Which vehicles could we do without?
Which vehicles pollute the air?

How does transport know where to go?

Each type of transport follows a route. Routes link different towns, cities and countries. Computers, cameras and satellites are used to monitor these routes and keep transport moving.

People drive cars and trucks along **roads**. Traffic lights, road signs and roundabouts help keep traffic moving.

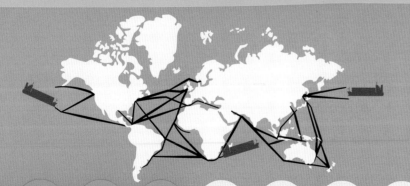

Even the captains of ships have to follow watery roads, called **shipping routes**. They were first created to help sailing ships take advantage of prevailing winds and ocean currents to move more quickly.

Think about ... how you would like to travel to different places.

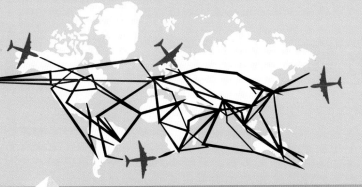

Aircraft fly along set **flight paths**. All flight times are recorded, so that airport controllers know that planes are flying to the right place at the right time. There can be up to 230,000 flights a day and up to 500,000 people in the air right now!

Gondola lifts carry skiers up mountains inside cabins connected to a loop of steel cable that turns around two giant pulley wheels.

Roads and railways work best when they go in a straight line, but sometimes they have to cross rivers and mountains. **Bridges** and **tunnels** span obstacles to make straight routes.

Boats sail up and down waterways called **canals**. The longest single canal, the Grand Canal in China, is 1,776 km in length with some sections dating back to the 5th century BCE. During the 18th and 19th centuries in Europe, canal boats moved goods along canals and rivers.

People use **maps** and **satellite navigation systems** to show them the best route and guide them to their destination.

Can you describe a route that you take?
Which route do you use to go the shops?
Can you draw a map of the route?

Which road signs do you see regularly?
Do you know what they mean?
How might it feel to ride in a gondola?

7

How many cars are there in the world?

The number of cars is growing all the time. It's estimated that there are around 1.3 billion. You could fit everyone in the world into cars if you squished five people into each one.

What was the first car?

Flywheel

What's the most popular car?

This beauty! The **Benz Patent Motor Car**, built in 1886. It looks like a bench on three wheels. You need to spin the flywheel at the back to get it started, steer with the front wheel rudder and stop it with the handbrake. It runs on petrol, but there were no petrol stations in 1886.

The **Toyota Corolla**. Forty-five million of them have been made since 1966 and they are still being built today. About 30,000 parts are needed to make each car, and a car can be built in 18 hours.

Think about ... how you would design a car.

What's the most expensive car?

The sleek **Bugatti La Voiture Noire** was sold for £14.4 million in 2019 and only one was ever made. It can go from 0 to 96.5 km/h in under 3 seconds. Hold tight!

Formula 1 cars race at speeds of 300 km/h, faster than a plane on take-off. As air moves over the car it creates drag, which keeps it on the ground. Grand Prix races are held each year, to find one world champion.

A problem with cars is the harmful emissions they produce. When petrol burns in a car engine it releases carbon dioxide (CO_2), a gas that causes global warming. Road transport accounts for 25 per cent of the world's CO_2.

What can we do about this?

It will help if we switch to **electric cars**, which don't release these harmful gases.

What's your favourite car?
What is the best shape for a car?
How have cars changed since 1886?

What features would you add to your car?
What renewable power sources could be used for cars? Solar power? Wind power?

How do you build roads?

Let's get involved and see ...

Roads have to be tough. They have to survive lots of wear and tear and need to last a long time, because repairing them stops the flow of traffic.

Making a road is like making a very crunchy layer cake. For the first layer, called the **subgrade**, an **excavator** is used to dig and level the ground. It removes rocks and boulders and then the soil is pressed as flat as possible.

A **tipper truck** adds a layer of crushed stones and sand, known as the **subbase**.

Think about ... which vehicles are needed to build roads.

A **bulldozer** is useful to spread the subbase across the road surface. The tiny gaps between the stones and sand allow the road surface to shrink in cold weather, and expand in hot weather.

The surface layer is made from sticky tar, gravel and sand. It's pressed smooth using a **steamroller**. In some countries, this layer is made of enormous slabs of poured concrete.

Now all we need are some roadside lights. A **cherry picker** lifts up a technician to put the bulbs in the lampposts.

Can you design a road-building vehicle?
What would it be like driving without roads?
When is the best time of day to repair a road?

What vehicles are not designed to be used on roads?
How can people make roads safer for wildlife?
How can you cross a road safely?

11

When was the wheel invented?

Wheels were invented around 3500 BCE. Evidence suggests that they were first used as potter's wheels before being used on chariots about 300 years later. The first wheels were solid discs of wood.

Wheels work better with an axle. An axle is a bar that connects two wheels together and allows them to spin freely. People living in Mesopotamia, which is modern-day Iraq, were the first to use a wheel axle for their horse-drawn chariots.

Potter's wheel

Axle

In 1888, John Boyd Dunlop invented the **pneumatic tyre,** a rubber tube filled with air. This reduces friction between the wheel and the road creating a smoother, more comfortable ride.

Trucks have the most wheels, usually around 18. The front axles have one wheel at each end, and the rest have two wheels at each end. More wheels means the weight of goods is shared between them. If one tyre blows, the others just keep on rolling.

Think about ... how wheels work.

Most passenger vehicles are two-wheel drive. This means the engine's power is only sent to the two front wheels, or the two back wheels.

Many people love watching truck drivers' skill at monster truck shows. The giant wheels help them to ramp, race and crush other cars. Monster trucks have four-wheel drive, where the engine sends power to all the wheels. This makes them more stable in ice and snow.

Here's a countdown of wheels on some vehicles that move people and packages around cities:

Taxis have four wheels. Yellow New York City taxis are easy to spot in traffic.

Auto rickshaws zip around cities on three wheels. Other names for them are tuk tuks or bajajes.

On two wheels, **motorbikes** and **scooters** whizz around, weaving in and out of traffic. They're useful for delivering packages super quickly.

Finally, on one wheel, here is the scary looking **Monowheel**. Do you think it would be easy to drive?

Why do different vehicles need different wheels and tyres? How does the tyre tread help cars to stay on the road?

What other wheeled vehicles can you think of? What would life be like without wheels?

How do trains work?

In many different ways! One of the earliest passenger trains was Stephenson's *Rocket*, built in 1829. It was powered by steam, created by boiling water. The steam pushed pistons, which made the wheels turn. It was hardly a fast rocket, though. The top speed was only 48 km/h.

Diesel engines

Diesel engines **suck** fuel into the piston cylinders.

Piston pushes up to **squeeze** the fuel.

Up and down motion becomes rotary motion.

The compressed fuel explodes - **bang!** It pushes the piston out, sucking more fuel in.

BANG!

After a hundred years, steam locomotives were slowly replaced by diesel locomotives. These allowed trains to travel faster and further. The largest was the **END DDA40X**, which ran on the Union Pacific railway in the USA. These trains had to carry their own diesel fuel, which made them even heavier.

UNION PACIFIC

Think about ... the different ways trains can be powered.

14

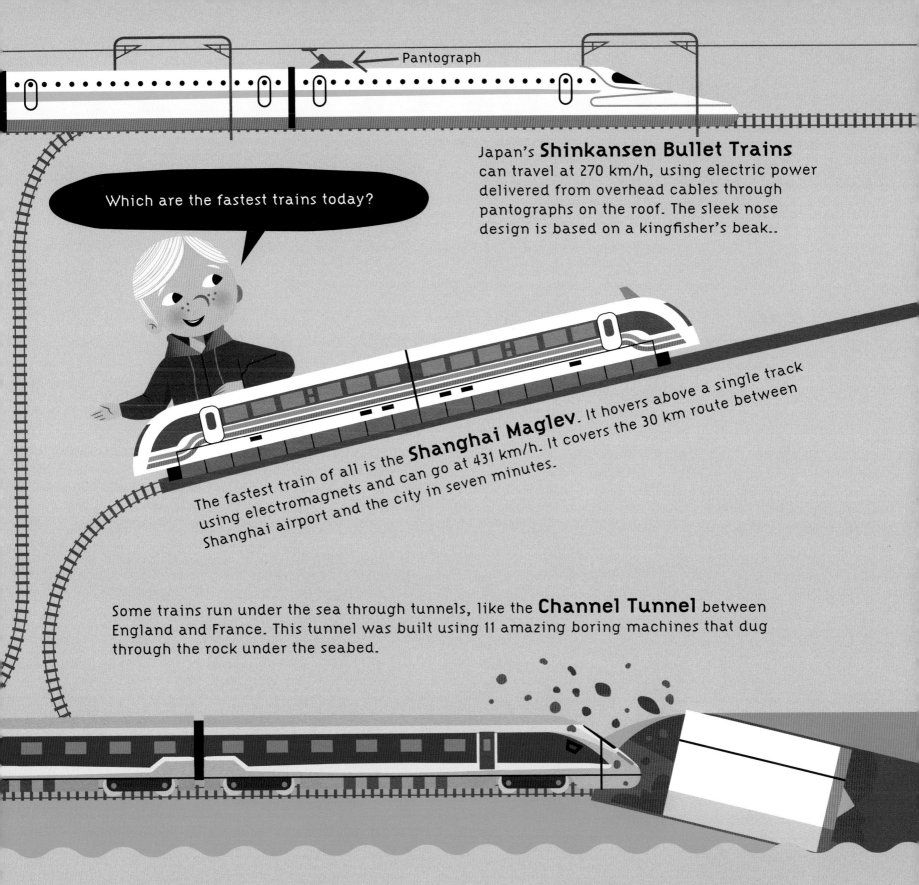

Pantograph

Japan's **Shinkansen Bullet Trains** can travel at 270 km/h, using electric power delivered from overhead cables through pantographs on the roof. The sleek nose design is based on a kingfisher's beak..

Which are the fastest trains today?

The fastest train of all is the **Shanghai Maglev**. It hovers above a single track using electromagnets and can go at 431 km/h. It covers the 30 km route between Shanghai airport and the city in seven minutes.

Some trains run under the sea through tunnels, like the **Channel Tunnel** between England and France. This tunnel was built using 11 amazing boring machines that dug through the rock under the seabed.

Which of these trains would you like to travel on?
Do you prefer car or train journeys?
Have you ever been on a steam train?

How would you improve trains?
Which speed would you be
happy to travel at on a train?

15

Why are there so many different types of boats?

Boats have been around for thousands of years. Rafts and canoes made from wood or reed have been found that are 8,000 years old. Today, we use boats to carry cargo, for fun holidays, to explore the seas, and trawl for fish. *Ship ahoy!*

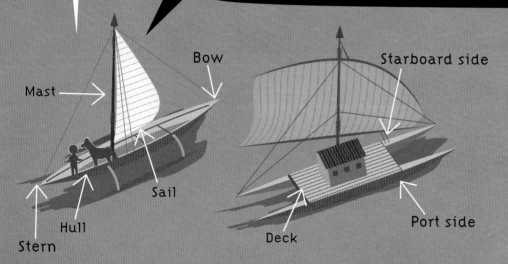

Mast

Bow

Starboard side

Sail

Hull

Stern

Deck

Port side

About 3,400 years ago, sailors reached Polynesia and started exploring islands in the Pacific Ocean. They sailed in **outrigger canoes** that had a float on one side for more stability. They developed double-hulled canoes for carrying explorers, settlers and their belongings. They were masters of navigation, using knowledge about the stars, wind and sea to guide their voyages.

When you want to move vast amounts of cargo to destinations all over the world, **container ships** are the solution. The largest container ships can carry almost 24,000 metal containers stuffed full of goodies.

Think about ... how many ships are sailing the seas at any one time.

Trawlers are ships that pull fishing nets behind the boat to scoop up fish. Fishermen use long lines with baited hooks, rather than nets, to catch tuna and swordfish. To protect fish and other ocean life, people set limits on where and when trawlers can work and how much fish they can catch.

Holidays on cruise ships are very popular. The *Symphony of the Seas*, launched in 2018, carries 6,680 passengers and 2,200 crew on 18 decks. For fun, it offers 23 swimming pools, laser tag and a huge slide.

Ferries are ships that can carry cars, lorries and passengers across rivers, lakes and seas. Roll-on roll-off ferries have doors on either end, so vehicles can drive in at one end and off the other.

The fastest motor-powered boat is the *Spirit of Australia*, which reached 511 km/h on Blowering Lake, Australia in 1978. It was built and driven by Ken Warby, who made it in his back yard.

How do boats stay afloat?
What shapes do all boats share?
What types of boats have you been on?

What materials are ships and boats made from?
What activities would you want on a cruise ship?
What would it be like living on a boat?

How do planes stay in the air?

It seems like magic, doesn't it? But it's not, it's the result of four different forces on the plane.

The plane's engine creates a thrust force driving the plane forward. This works against the drag force that holds the plane back. When the thrust is stronger than the drag, the plane moves forward.

The weight of the plane holds it to the ground, but once there is enough speed in the forward thrust, a lift force is created by air passing over and under the wings. Once the lift force is stronger than the weight force, the plane will take off. Easy!

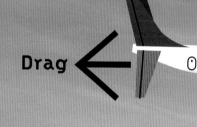

Lift

Drag

Thrust

Weight

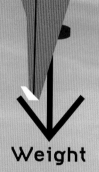

The **Wright *Flyer*** was the first powered plane in the world. It took off in December 1903, the flight lasted just 12 seconds but was a triumph for the inventors, Wilbur and Orville Wright.

Think about ... whether people should continue taking flights.

18

The **Airbus A380** is the biggest passenger plane in the world. It can carry 853 passengers at a time. It also flies the longest commercial route of any plane – 15,770 km in 17 hours from Sydney, Australia to Dallas, USA.

Aircrafts with jet engines are very bad for the environment, because they use up a lot of fuel very quickly. We need different ways to power planes. The **Cessna Caravan** is the largest all-electric aircraft, but it can only carry nine people, and fly for 30 minutes.

Solar Impulse 2 is powered by the Sun. It uses 17,000 photovoltaic cells, like those on solar panels, to gather energy from the Sun. It can fly at speeds of about 48 km/h, or faster if the Sun is bright.

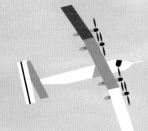

The biggest cargo plane in the world is the Antonov **AN-225 Mriya**. It has six jet engines and can carry up to 250,000 kg of cargo. The whole nose cone flips up so that cars or other cargo can get inside.

What other machines can fly? How many flights do you think you will take in your life?

Have you ever been on a plane? What did it feel like? How is the Wright *Flyer* the same, or different, to the Airbus A380?

19

How do rockets get into space?

To enter space, rockets need to move upwards really quickly with lots of power to escape Earth's gravity.

The **payload** holds the astronauts and cargo.

Moving at 28,000 km/h, it takes 10 minutes to leave Earth's atmosphere.

The **second stage** has one engine and enough fuel to steer the payload into the correct orbit.

The rocket burns loads of fuel and liquid oxygen really quickly, producing hot gas that shoots out of the back.

This gas pushes against the ground, forcing the rocket up.

The **first stage** propulsion system carries the fuel and oxygen. Once the fuel is burnt up, this section is released and drops to the ground.

Think about ... where you would send a rocket.

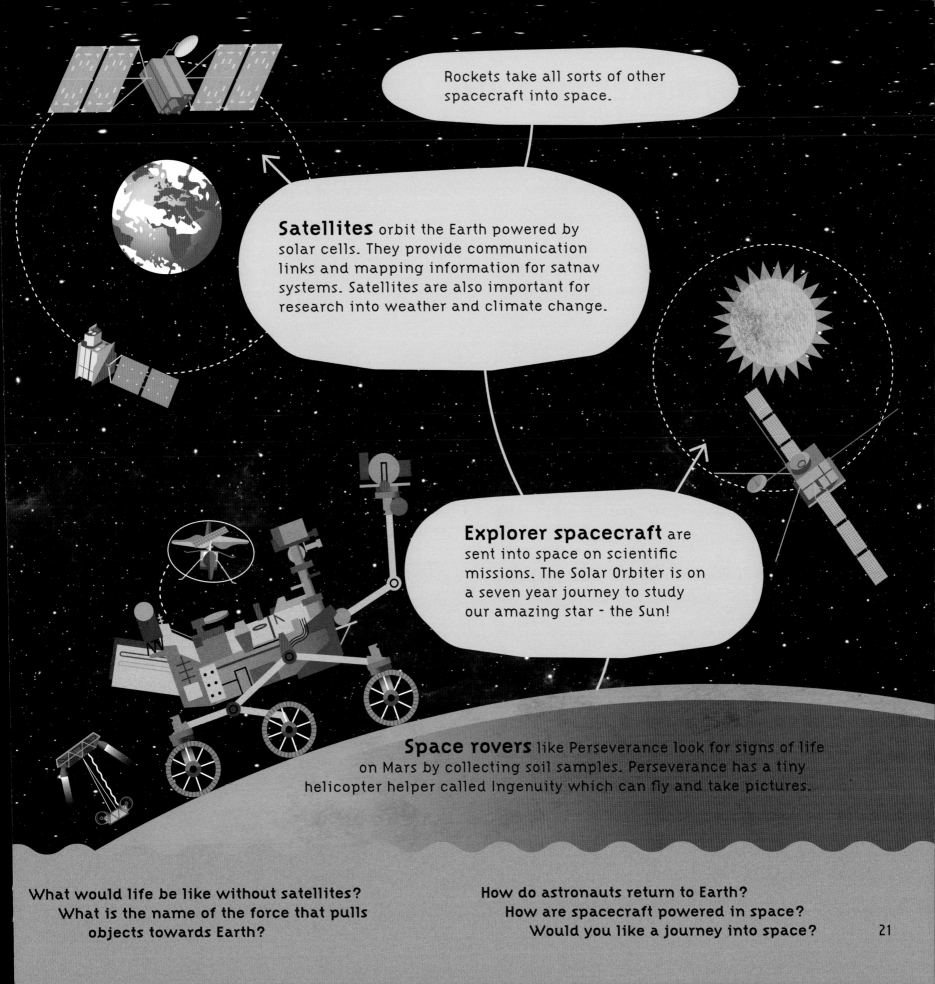

Rockets take all sorts of other spacecraft into space.

Satellites orbit the Earth powered by solar cells. They provide communication links and mapping information for satnav systems. Satellites are also important for research into weather and climate change.

Explorer spacecraft are sent into space on scientific missions. The Solar Orbiter is on a seven year journey to study our amazing star - the Sun!

Space rovers like Perseverance look for signs of life on Mars by collecting soil samples. Perseverance has a tiny helicopter helper called Ingenuity which can fly and take pictures.

What would life be like without satellites?
What is the name of the force that pulls objects towards Earth?

How do astronauts return to Earth?
How are spacecraft powered in space?
Would you like a journey into space?

What vehicles help us?

There are many emergency vehicles that can help if there is an accident. We can call for help on emergency telephone numbers. Brave and expert drivers bring the vehicles to the scene to help.

Police cars have powerful engines so that drivers can respond quickly to an emergency. They also have flashing lights on top and a loud siren that tells other drivers to pull over and let them through.

Most **fire engines** can carry up to eight firefighters and lots of equipment. On the back is a ladder that can turn and extend to reach high windows. Firefighters attach the fire hose to the tank on the fire engine or to the main water supply to put out a fire.

Think about ... how you would design a new rescue vehicle.

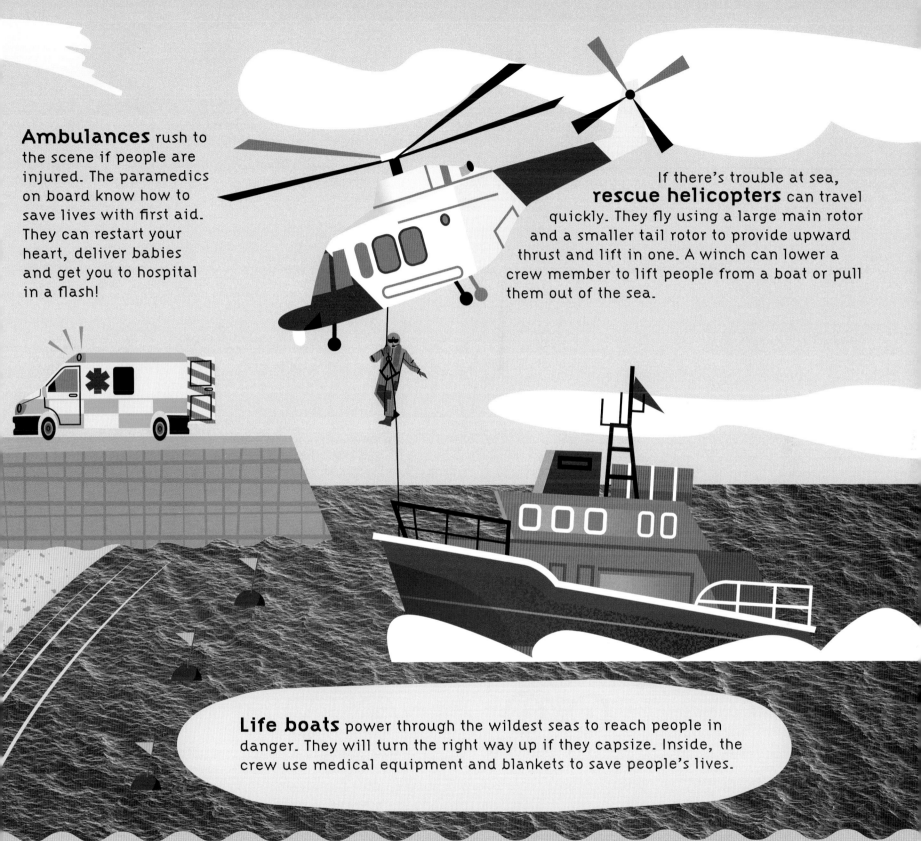

Ambulances rush to the scene if people are injured. The paramedics on board know how to save lives with first aid. They can restart your heart, deliver babies and get you to hospital in a flash!

If there's trouble at sea, **rescue helicopters** can travel quickly. They fly using a large main rotor and a smaller tail rotor to provide upward thrust and lift in one. A winch can lower a crew member to lift people from a boat or pull them out of the sea.

Life boats power through the wildest seas to reach people in danger. They will turn the right way up if they capsize. Inside, the crew use medical equipment and blankets to save people's lives.

Which emergency vehicles have you seen? Which emergency vehicle could help if you were stuck up a tall tree?

What can a helicopter do that a plane cannot? Which of these vehicles is driven by a pilot? How does a fire hose work?

23

What forms of transport can kids use?

There are loads of vehicles that kids can use to get around. Bicycles are really popular. Here's a quick history of the bicycle in pictures ...

1818 - Hobby horse
A no-pedals running machine with wheels.

1850 - Tricycle
Three-wheelers became popular for a while.

1860 - Velocipede
The 'boneshaker' had pedals attached to the front wheel.

1870 - Penny farthing
A very popular bike. Thomas Stevens cycled round the world on one in 1884.

1885 - Safety bike
Pedals connected to the back wheel with a chain meant smaller wheels

1890s - Cheaper bikes
Cheaper bikes meant more women could buy them and live freer lives.

1900s - Bike gears
Gears added to bikes made cycling easier.

1920s onwards - Children's bikes
Bikes became a popular toy for children.

1953 - Woodsie
The first mountain bike was built.

1970s - Carbon fibre
Light, strong carbon fibre used to make racing bikes.

2000 - Electric bike
Pedalling stores energy in a battery fitted to an electric bike, to power riders up hills.

Today - Bikes for all
There is a bike out there for road riding, stunts, hurtling down hills or racing.

Think about ... what vehicles you like to use.

Skateboards are a simple vehicle first made in the 1940s. Today, there are around 11 million skateboarders and it has even become an Olympic sport! Riding on ramps achieves enough speed to perform tricks and jumps.

Don't forget you can transport yourself with **walking** or **running** power, or in a **wheelchair**. It's important to keep moving to stay healthy.

Kick scooters have two or three wheels, a deck and handlebar to grip and steer. They're great for getting around and for practising tricks, like a fakie or a tail whip.

Bearings

Some kids like to ride horses.

I do!

Roller skates have been around since 1819. Skate wheels have small metal balls in them called bearings that make them roll smoother and faster.

What special features would your ideal bike have? Do you think cyclists should have special routes, to keep them safe?

What other vehicles can kids use? Why should you wear a helmet when you scoot, skate or cycle?

Cleaner

Transport will use cleaner energy, such as electric or solar power.

There may be smaller vehicles that use less power.

People may own vehicles jointly.

What will transport be like in the future?

Let's think ...

Driverless

There might be computer-controlled cars. trucks, buses, planes, trains and boats that don't need humans to drive them.

Less travel?

Will we need to travel so much?

Will we shop online and have robots deliver our shopping?

Will we get all our lessons and work through a computer or tablet?

Think about ... transport of the future.

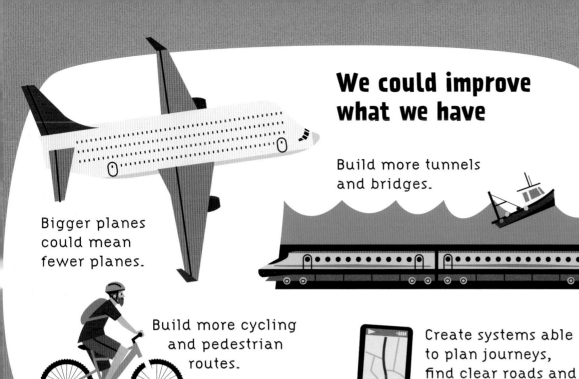

We could improve what we have

Bigger planes could mean fewer planes.

Build more tunnels and bridges.

Build more cycling and pedestrian routes.

Create systems able to plan journeys, find clear roads and parking spaces.

Better mobility

Improved transport for disabled and elderly people.

Cheaper, better wheelchairs and mobility scooters ...

and robotic suits to help with walking.

Healthy humans and healthy planet

More journeys taken by foot or cycle.

Street lighting that switches on only when needed.

Electric-powered public transport.

Machines that record emissions, to encourage responsibility for the environment.

It's over to you — the future of transport is in your hands.
What transport can you imagine and design for the future?

Many more questions!

1. How many yellow cars can you find in the book?

2. What year did the Wright *Flyer* take off? How many years ago was that?

3. Why are cars harmful to the environment?

4. What is Perseverance doing on Mars?

5. What vehicle would you use to put bulbs in a lamppost?

6. How many rotors does a helicopter have?

7. How many passengers can the Airbus A380 carry?

8. How many wheels would three tuk-tuks and four motorbikes have?

9. Where is the longest canal? How long is it?

10. What's your favourite form of transport? Why?

Further information

Websites

facts.kiddle.co/Transport

www.howstuffworks.com

www.sciencekids.co.nz/sciencefacts/vehicles.html

Books

Awesome Engineering: Trains, Planes and Ships by Sally Spray (2019), Franklin Watts

Code: STEM: Transport by Max Wainewright (2020), Wayland

Kid Engineer: Working with Transport by Sonya Newland (2020), Wayland

Glossary

Atmosphere – the thick layer of gases that surrounds Earth

Billion – 1,000,000,000 – one thousand million

Cargo – goods carried by boat or plane

CO$_2$ – short for carbon dioxide, a gas released when vehicle engines burn fuel or animals breathe out

Commercial – connected with business and the buying and selling of goods and services

Drag (force) – a force that slows down a moving object as it moves through air or liquid

Electromagnet – a piece of metal that becomes a very strong magnet when electricity is passed through it

Emissions – making and sending out heat, light, gases etc

Fakie – a skateboard trick involving riding the board backwards

Flywheel – a wheel within a machine that keeps an engine running smoothly

Force – a push or a pull.

Friction – a force that slows down motion as two surfaces move over each other

Global warming – the increase in the temperature of Earth's atmosphere

Goods – things that are made or grown to be sold, such as clothes, machines or food

Gravity – a force that pulls objects towards each other. Earth's gravity pulls everything towards the centre of Earth

Hull – the main part of a boat that rests in the water

Jet engine – an engine that moves a plane forwards by pushing a stream of gases out behind it

Lift (force) – the upward force produced by the wing of a plane. The shape of the wing makes air travel faster over the top of the wing than underneath the wing, creating lift

Obstacle – an object blocking the way

Ocean current – the movement of water flowing in one direction

Pantograph – a piece of equipment on the roof of an electric train used to pass electricity from an overhead wire to the train engine

Paramedic – a person trained in emergency medicine who works from an ambulance

Photovoltaic cells – a cell that collects sunlight and converts it into electricity

Piston – a part of an engine that moves up and down (or backwards and forwards) inside a tube to make other parts of the engine move

Pneumatic – filled with air

Potter's wheel – a wheel used to help potters shape clay

Pollute – to add dirty substances to water or air

Polynesia – a large group of islands in the Pacific Ocean

Prevailing – prevailing winds are the winds that usually blow around the world

Pulley – a wheel, often one of a pair, that is used with ropes or chains to pull or lift heavy objects

Renewable – renewable power is power generated using natural resources, such as the power of the wind or moving water, that will not run out

Rotor – moving in a circle around a point

Rudder – a piece of metal or wood that is moved to help steer a boat or other vehicle

Satellite – an artificial satellite is a man-made device, sent into space in order to gather or transmit information

Satnav/satellite navigation – a computer system that uses information gathered from satellites to guide the driver of a vehicle

Solar – connected to the Sun

Tread – the pattern on tyres that help vehicles grip the road

Thrust (force) – a push force which moves planes through air or moves other vehicles on land

Game cards

You can play with the game cards in a number of ways:
Choose a transport card and get a friend to ask questions that you can answer with a yes or no, e.g. Does it have wheels?
They can guess the transport card through a process of elimination.

Name Horse
Description
4 legged galloper

Length 2 m
Speed 54 km/h
Cool factor 9
Ability score 3

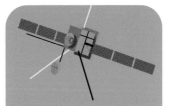

Name Solar Orbiter
Description
Sun-observing satellite

Length 2.5 m
Speed 700,000 km/h
Cool factor 10
Ability score 8

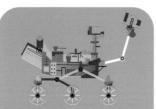

Name Perseverance
Description
Marvellous Mars Rover

Length 3 m
Speed 0.15 km/h
Cool factor 9
Ability score 8

Name X-15
Description
World's fastest plane

Length 15 m
Speed 7,274 km/h
Cool factor 7
Ability score 8

Name Bulldozer
Description
Heavy earth mover

Length 8.1 m
Speed 10 km/h
Cool factor 2
Ability score 6

Name Penny Farthing
Description
Lopsided wheel bike

Length 1.7 m
Speed 28 km/h
Cool factor 6
Ability score 4

Name Runner
Description
2 legged galloper

Length 1.6 m
Speed 10 km/h
Cool factor 4
Ability score 2

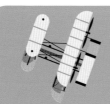

Name Wright Flyer
Description
First fantastic flyer

Length 6.4 m
Speed 48 km/h
Cool factor 7
Ability score 3

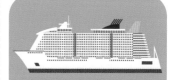

Name Cruise Ship
Description
Huge holiday ship

Length 362 m
Speed 41 km/h
Cool factor 7
Ability score 7

Name Cessna Caravan
Description
Electric aircraft

Length 11 m
Speed 344 km/h
Cool factor 8
Ability score 4

Name Rescue helicopter
Description
Hovering helper

Length 17 m
Speed 306 km/h
Cool factor 7
Ability score 8

Name Canal boat
Description
Waterway load carrier

Length 22 m
Speed 6.4 km/h
Cool factor 4
Ability score 2

Name Toyota Corolla
Description
Most popular car

Length 4.6 m
Speed 180 km/h
Cool factor 5
Ability score 5

Name Benz Patent
Motor Car
Description First Car

Length 2.5 m
Speed 16 km/h
Cool factor 9
Ability score 3

Name Electric car
Description
Plug in car

Length 4 m
Speed 150 km/h
Cool factor 8
Ability score 6

Photograph or scan the cards, print them, cut them out and you can play the following games:
- Top Trumps
- Snap (you will need to print out two sets of cards)
- Lotto (you will need to print out two sets of cards)
- Matching pairs (you will need to print out two sets of cards).

Create your own transport cards to add to the pack.

Name
Bugatti La Voiture Noire
Description
Most expensive car

Length 4.5 m
Speed 420 km/h
Cool factor 10
Ability score 10

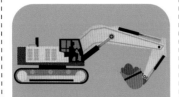

Name Excavator
Description
Long armed digger

Length 18 m
Speed 10 km/h
Cool factor 4
Ability score 7

Name Kids Scooter
Description
Foot push powered

Length 1 m
Speed 16 km/h
Cool factor 5
Ability score 2

Name Monster Truck
Description
Big wheel boss

Length 5 m
Speed 161 km/h
Cool factor 9
Ability score 8

Name New York Taxi
Description
Yellow icon

Length 5.3 m
Speed 11 km/h
Cool factor 7
Ability score 4

Name Motorbike
Description
2 wheeled whizzer

Length 2 m
Speed 300 km/h
Cool factor 8
Ability score 9

Name Monowheel
Description
1 wheeled wonder

Length 1.7 m
Speed 98 km/h
Cool factor 7
Ability score 1

Name Tuk-tuk
Description
Three wheeled taxi

Length 2.6 m
Speed 30 km/h
Cool factor 5
Ability score 3

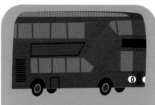

Name Bus
Description
Double trouble

Length 13 m
Speed 50 km/h
Cool factor 7
Ability score 5

Name
Stephenson's Rocket
Description First
passenger steam train

Length 4 m
Speed 48 km/h
Cool factor 7
Ability score 7

Name EMD DDA40X
Description
Mighty diesel train

Length 30 m
Speed 145 km/h
Cool factor 6
Ability score 6

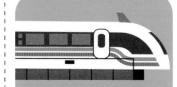

Name Shanghai Maglev
Description Speedy
commuter train

Length 153 m
Speed 431 km/h
Cool factor 9
Ability score 10

Name Car Ferry
Description
Rockin' roll on roll off

Length 209 m
Speed 35 km/h
Cool factor 5
Ability score 5

Name Life Boat
Description All-weather
rescue boat

Length 14 m
Speed 46 km/h
Cool factor 7
Ability score 9

Name Police Car
Description Rapid
response vehicle

Length 4.7 m
Speed 155 km/h
Cool factor 8
Ability score 9

Index